The Best Bible
Coloring & Activity Book
with fun-filled reproducible pages™

Copyright ©2017 GiGi Allen

G†G

Glory to God Publications

I Love My Bible

Do not let this Book of the Law depart from your mouth;
meditate on it day and night,
so that you may be careful to do everything written in it.
Then you will be prosperous and successful.
Joshua 1:8

Animals in the Bible Crossword

Across

1. Swallowed Jonah
2. Peter denied Jesus then…
3. Rise Peter kill and eat (God made clean)
4. Bird
5. The wise men rode on a _____

Down

1. Baby sheep
2. Jesus rode on a _____
3. Needs a shepherd.
4. Prepares for winter, called wise in Proverbs 6:6.
5. Daniel killed one.
6. Likes climbing mountains.
7. Type of black bird
8. Returned to Noah with an olive branch.
9. _____ of Judah.

2

BE DEVOTED TO ONE ANOTHER IN BROTHERLY LOVE.

Honor one another above yourselves.

Romans 12:9

Love is ...
Word Search

```
H  J  U  R  G  J  Q  R  Z  P  D  P  J  B  C  R  K  R  R  J  N
G  I  O  T  G  P  F  T  A  D  A  D  D  P  T  T  L  T  A  P  H
R  S  P  O  P  S  O  O  J  S  G  S  R  P  P  A  J  O  L  S  A
T  U  D  J  D  U  S  J  P  F  P  F  T  A  D  J  R  J  E  U  K
G  O  P  P  S  S  H  P  S  D  R  D  O  T  S  P  S  K  I  N  D
C  T  F  D  F  T  F  D  U  K  O  K  J  I  F  D  U  D  F  T  S
A  S  D  S  D  S  R  S  E  H  T  S  P  E  D  S  K  S  P  S  H
G  L  K  U  K  L  E  U  A  T  E  T  D  N  N  U  T  U  D  L  I
E  J  S  D  S  J  J  S  S  C  C  C  S  T  E  S  S  L  P  J  E
L  R  T  T  T  R  O  T  L  T  T  J  U  R  V  T  N  T  E  R  P
S  D  C  S  C  D  I  F  E  V  S  V  S  D  E  C  O  C  R  D  S
L  N  J  S  J  B  C  A  R  B  R  B  T  B  R  S  T  S  S  B  T
C  O  V  L  V  T  E  I  D  R  D  R  C  T  F  L  P  B  E  T  C
S  T  V  J  B  R  S  T  O  D  B  D  S  R  A  J  R  J  V  R  S
L  R  R  E  R  P  R  H  T  C  T  C  L  P  I  V  O  V  E  F  L
J  U  D  B  N  O  D  B  L  H  O  P  E  O  L  B  U  N  R  O  L
V  D  C  R  C  B  C  R  P  X  P  X  V  R  S  R  D  R  E  R  V
R  E  O  S  T  E  R  D  O  Z  O  Z  T  N  O  Y  K  K  S  O  D
```

Love is patient, love is kind...Love never fails. 1 Corinthians 13:4-8

LOVE	REJOICES
FAITH	PROTECTS
HOPE	TRUSTS
PATIENT	PERSEVERES
KIND	NOT PROUD
NOT RUDE	NEVER FAILS

I CAN DO EVERYTHING

through him who gives me strength.

Philippians 4:13

Scripture Scramble

___ ___ ___ ___ ___ ___
oHw   tgear   si   eht   velo   eht

___ ___ ___ ___ ___
Freath   ash   dehsival   no   su

___ ___ ___ ___ ___
ttah   ew   dluohs   eb   llaedc

___ ___ ___! ___ ___
nerdlihc   fo   odG   ndA   hatt

___ ___ ___ ___!   1 John 3:1
si   tahw   ew   rea

6

PRAISE THE LORD

I will extol the LORD at all times; his praise will always be on my lips.
Glorify the LORD with me; let us exalt his name together.

Psalm 34:1,3

Word Challenge

How many words can you make out of

trust in the Lord?

hen		
tent		

Trust in the LORD with all your heart and lean not on your own understanding; in all your ways acknowledge him, and he will make your paths straight. Proverbs 3:5-6

8

But the fruit of the Spirit is

LOVE, JOY,

peace,

PATIENCE,

kindness, goodness, faithfulness, gentleness and

SELF-CONTROL

Galatians 5:22-23

9

Books of the Bible Crossword

Across
1. The letters mixed up: hiiiPPPlans
2. The 17th book of the New Testament
3. The book before Revelations
4. Between Ephesians and Timothy
5. The letters mixed up: aaasnitlg

Down
1. Starts with P, ends with n
2. Follows Ezekiel
3. Two books before Colossians
4. Follows Philemon

...for the joy of the Lord is your strength.

Nehemiah 8:10

11

Compassion Word Search

```
H K U R G J Q R L O V P J B C R K R R J N
G I O T L P F T A D T D D P T G R A C E H
R K P I O S I O J S G S R S P A J O L S A
T I D J V U S J P F P F T U D J B J E U K
G N P M S S H P S D S D O S S P S L N S E
C D F D E T F D U F L L J T F D U D E T S
A N D S D R D S E O S S O S D S K S D S H
G E K U K L C U A R V T D V K U T U K L S
E S S C S J S Y B G S C S J E S S L S J E
L S T O T R T T L I L J U R T T L T R P
S D C M C D C C E V J V S D C C J G C D S
T B J P J B J S R E R B T B D S R E J B T
C T V A V T V L N D R C T L L D N V T C
S R L S E R V E O E B D S R V J B E U R S
L P R S R P R V T S T C L P E V T R R F L
J O D I N O D B L S R V J O D B R O O O L
V R C O C B C R P X P X V R C R P U C R V
R L O N T E R D O Z O Z T N O Y K S N O D
```

GRACE
MERCY
COMPASSION
FORGIVENESS
LOVE
GENEROUS
BLESS
SERVE
KINDNESS

The Lord is full of compassion and mercy. James 5:11

LOVE IS PATIENT, LOVE IS KIND.

1 Corinthians 13:4

Scripture Scramble

_____ _____ _____ ___ ___ _____ ___
tBu   het   tiurf   fo   eth   tiirpS   si

_____, ____, _____, _____,
velo   oyj   apeec   ecnetapi

_____, _____, _____,
nessdnki   noossegd   ssffeuanlthi

_____ ____ _____-_____.
eeessnnltg   nad   lesf   oonrtlc

Galatians 5:22-23

Dear friends, since God so loved us, we also ought to

LOVE ONE ANOTHER.

1 John 4:11

Word Challenge

How many words can you make out of

we are God's workmanship?

man	ape	pig
___	___	___
___	___	___
___	___	___
___	___	___
___	___	___
___	___	___
___	___	___
___	___	___
___	___	___

For we are God's workmanship, created in Christ Jesus to do good works, which God prepared in advance for us to do. Ephesians 2:10

16

LOVE NEVER FAILS.

1 Corinthians 13:8

17

Noah's Ark Crossword

Across
1. Pets
2. Who built the ark?
3. Another word for promise.
4. What book of the Bible says God created the animals?
5. Hebrews 11:7 By _____ Noah...

Down
1. Came with a promise
2. Huge animal
3. Boat
4. Like a big cat

18

THE TONGUE HAS THE POWER OF LIFE AND DEATH... PROVERBS 18:21

Do not let any unwholesome talk come out of your mouths, but only what is helpful for building others up according to their needs, that it may benefit those who listen.
Ephesians 4:29

Think on These Things
Word Search

```
H J U R G J Q R Z P D P J B C R K R R J N
G I O T G P F T A D E N D P T T L T A P H
R S P I P S I O R S G S O S P A J O L S A
T U D J D U S J P U P F T B D J R J E U K
G O P P S S H P S D E D O S L P U R E S P
C T T D F T F D U K X K J T F E U D F T R
A S H S D S D S E H C S P S D A K S D S A
G L I U K L K U A T E T D L K C T U K L I
E J N D S J S S B C L C S J S E S L S J S
L R K T T A T T L J L J U R T O L T T R E
S D C S C D C C E V E V S D C F J C C D W
T B J S J M J S R B N B T B D G R S J B O
C T V L V I V R D R T R C L L O D B V T R
S R L J B R B J I D D D S O V D B J U R T
L P R A R A R V T G B C L V E V T V R F H
J O D B N B D B L V H V J E D B R N O O Y
V R C R C L C R P X R T V L C R P R C R C
R L O I T E R D O Z P Z T Y O Y K K N O O
```

Finally, brothers, whatever is true, whatever is noble, whatever is right, whatever is pure, whatever is lovely, whatever is admirable – if anything Is excellent or praiseworthy – think about such things. Philippians 4:8

TRUE   ADMIRABLE
NOBLE   EXCELLENT
RIGHT   PRAISEWORTHY
PURE   PEACE OF GOD
LOVELY   THINK

20

LiVe TOGeTHeR iN UNiTY

How good and pleasant it is when God's people live together in unity!
Psalm 133:1

21

Scripture Scramble

_____ _____ _____ _____ _____ _____ _____
oD otn tel thsi kBoo fo eth

_____ _____ _____ _____ _____ ;
Lwa traped rmof ryuo thmou

_____ _____ _____ _____ _____ _____ ,
ettidem a no ti yad nad ghtni

_____ _____ _____ _____ _____ _____
os ttah uoy yma eb ecarluf

_____ _____ _____ _____ _____ _____
ot od gnhtyrviee rwentti ni

___ . _____ _____ _____ _____
ti neTh ouy liwl eb

_____ _____ _____ . Joshua 1:8
ssuoorrepp dna fulsscceu

You, my brothers, were called to be free...
SERVE ONE ANOTHER IN LOVE.
Galatians 5:13

23

Word Challenge

How many words can you make out of

forgive others?

frog   hot

_____   _____   _____

_____   _____   _____

_____   _____   _____

_____   _____   _____

_____   _____   _____

_____   _____   _____

_____   _____   _____

_____   _____   _____

For if you forgive men when they sin against you, your heavenly Father will also forgive you. But if you do not forgive men their sins, your Father will not forgive your sins. Matthew 6:14-15

Give thanks to the God of heaven.

HIS LOVE ENDURES FOREVER.

Psalm 136:26
And so we know and rely on the love God has for us. God is love.
1 John 4:16

Books of the Bible Crossword

Down
1. Mixed up: SNAMOR
2. Ends with S
3. Mixed up: SSSAANNIOLHTE
4. Follows Romans

Across
1. Last book of the Bible
2. Starts with T
3. Starts with J
4. Disciple walked on water
5. Matthew, Mark, Luke, ___

26

GOD MADE ME

I praise you because I am...
wonderfully made... Psalm 139:14

Joshua 1:8 Word Search

```
B J U R G J Q R Z P D P J O C R K R R J T
I I O T G P F T A D E D D B T T L T A P W
B S P I P S I O J S G S R E P A J O L S R
L U D J D N S J P E V E R Y T J R J E U I
G O P P S S I P S D S D O S H P S P N S T
C T F D F T F G U K U K J T I D U D F T T
A S D S D S D S H H S S P S N S K S D S E
G L K U K B K U A T V T D L G U T U P L N
E J S D S I S S B C S C S J T S S L R J I
L R T T T B T T L J L J U R C T U T O R M
S D C S C L C C H V J V S D D C C C S D E
T B J S J E J J R E R B T B L S C S P B D
C T V L V T V O D R N R C T V L E B E T I
S R L J B R B S O D B D S R E J S J R R T
L P R A R P R H T C T C L P D V S V O F A
D O D B N O D U L V R V J O C B F N U O T
V A C R C B C A P X P X V R O R U R S R E
R L Y I T E R D O Z O Z T N T Y L K T O L
```

Do not let this Book of the Law depart from your mouth; meditate on it day
and night, so that you may be careful to do everything written in it.
Then you will be prosperous and successful. Joshua 1:8

BIBLE
MEDITATE
DAY
NIGHT
OBEY
EVERYTHING

WRITTEN
THEN
PROSPEROUS
SUCCESSFUL
JOSHUA

28

GOD LOVES US!

How great is the love the Father has lavished on us

1 John 3:1

Scripture Scramble

_____ ___ ___ _____ ____
Ttah   fi   ouy   fesscon   ithw

____ _____, " ____ __ ____,"
ruoy   thoum   ssJue   si   droL

___ _____ __ ____ _____
dna   eeelbiv   ni   uory   arthe

____ ___ _____ ___ ____
hatt   doG   asiedr   mih   omfr

___ ____ ___ ____ __
hte   aedd   uoy   llwi   eb

_____.   **Romans 10:9**
daves

30

LOVE.... IT ALWAYS PROTECTS.

1 Corinthians 13:7

31

Word Challenge

How many words can you make out of
therefore love is the fulfillment of the law?

__lion__ __ _____ __ _____

__ _____ __ _____ __ _____

__ _____ __ _____ __ _____

__ _____ __ _____ __ _____

__ _____ __ _____ __ _____

__ _____ __ _____ __ _____

__ _____ __ _____ __ _____

__ _____ __ _____ __ _____

**"Love your neighbor as yourself." Love does no harm to its neighbor.
Therefore love is the fulfillment of the law. Romans 13:9-10**

LOVE NEVER FAILS.

1 Corinthians 13:8

Apostles Crossword

Down
1. Doubting _____
2. Starts with B
3. Gave Jesus a kiss

Across
1. He wrote "the disciple Jesus loved"
2. Starts with A, ends ends with W
3. The letters mixed up: DDAAEUSHT
4. Another name for Peter
5. In the book of _____ we're told to control our tongue.
6. The first book of the New Testament.

Whatever you do,
WORK AT IT WITH ALL YOUR HEART,
as working for the Lord...

Colossians 3:23

35

Genesis Chapter 1
Word Search

```
H J U R G J Q R Z P D P J B C R K A R J N
G O D T G P F T A E V E D P T G L T D P H
R S P O P S O O J S G S R L P A J O L A A
T U D J D U S J P F P F N A D R R J E C M
G O P P S S H P S D S D I N S D S P N R E
C T F D F T F D U K G K G T F E U D F E S
A S D S D S D S G H E S H S D N K S D A H
G L K U D L K U O T N T T J G U T U K T I
E J S D S A S S O C E C S R O S S L S E E
L R T T T R Y T D J S J U D D T L C T D P
R D C S C L C C D V I V S B S C J R C D S
U B J S J I J S O B S B T T A S R E J G T
L T V L V K V L T R D R C R I L D A V E C
E R L J B E B I L D B D S I D J B T U N S
O P R A R N R G L C T I L P D V T U R E L
V O D B N E D H L V R V R O C B R R O S L
E R C R C S C T P X P X V D O R P E C I V
R F I S H S R D I M A G E N S Y K S N T D
```

GOD	RULE OVER
CREATED	FISH
ADAM	BIRDS
EVE	CREATURES
GARDEN	PLANTS
GOD SAID	DAY
LIGHT	NIGHT
IMAGE	GOOD
LIKENESS	GENESIS

36

Be completely humble
and gentle;
Be patient,
bearing with one another
in love.
Ephesians 4:2

Scripture Scramble

_____, _____ _____ ___
Fllyain   srethrob   eearvthw   si

_____, _____ ___ _____,
erut   revetahw   si   oenbl

_____ ___ _____, _____
twhrveea   si   gthri   raeevwht

___ _____, _____ ___ _____
si   uerp   eearvthw   si   eylvlo

_____ ___ _____ _-___
revewhta   si   elbarimad   fi

_____ ___ _____ ___
ygnnthai   si   eeellxctn   ro

_____-_____ _____ ____ ____ _____
ythrowpeisar   tkinh   atbuo   hcus   gsnhti

Philippians 4:8

BLESS MY FOOD

Worship the LORD your God,
and his blessing will be on your food and water.
Exodus 23:25

...it is consecrated by the word of God and prayer.
1 Timothy 4:5

Word Challenge

How many words can you make out of
with God all things are possible?

dog	bone	star
___	___	___
___	___	___
___	___	___
___	___	___
___	___	___
___	___	___
___	___	___
___	___	___
___	___	___

Jesus looked at them and said, "With man this is impossible, but with God all things are possible." Matthew 19:26

40

That if you confess with your mouth "Jesus is Lord," and believe in your heart that God raised him from the dead, you shall be saved... Romans 10:9

New Testament Books of the Bible Crossword

Down

1. Starts with M
2. Ends with S
3. _____, Philemon, Hebrews, James
4. The 65th book of the Bible

Across

1. Ends with K
2. Follows the book of John
3. A language plus S
4. Before the book of Acts
5. Gospels, Acts, _____
6. Starts with G

love is kind. 1 Corinthians 13:4

43

Faith Word Search

```
H J U H G J Q R Z W A L K B Y F A I T H N
E H O E G P F T A D A D D P T T L T A P O
B S P O P S O O J S G S R S P A J O L S T
R U D J D U S J P F P F H U D J R J E U B
G H P P S S H P S D S T P S J P S P N S Y
C E F D F T F D U K I K L T F E U D F T S
A B D S D S E S E A S S E W D S S S D S I
G R K U K L V U F T V T A O K U T U K L G
E E S D S J I S B C S A S R S S S L S J H
L W T T T R D T L J L B E D T L T T T S T
S S C S C D E C E V J R S O C C J C C U S
T B J S J B N S R B R A G F D S R E J B T
C T V L V T C L D R D H O G L L D R V S W
S R L J B R E J O D B A D O V J B T U T S
L P R A R P R V T C T M L D E V T A R A L
H O P E N O D B L V R V J O D B R I O N L
V R C R C B C R P X P X V R C R P N C C V
R L O A T E R D O Z O Z T N O Y K K N E W
```

Now faith is being sure of what we hope for and certain of what we do not see. Hebrews 11:1

FAITH   HOPE
HEBREWS   CERTAIN
WORD OF GOD   SUBSTANCE
PLEASES GOD   EVIDENCE
WALK BY FAITH   JESUS
NOT BY SIGHT   ABRAHAM

I believe the Word of God

...Give God a Tenth...

Luke 11:42

Mal. 3:10; Deut. 14:22; Prov. 3:9;
Matt. 23:23; 2 Cor. 9:6; Luke 18:12;
Prov. 8:18

45

Scripture Scramble

___ ___ ___ _____
eB   dkin   nda   passateioncom

____ _____ _____, _____
ot   noe   otheran   ro ggii vnf

_____ _____, _____ ____ ____
aehc   thore   tjus   sa   ni

_____ _____ _____ _____.
sCrhti   oGd   evagrof   ouy

Ephesians 4:32

46

GOD CREATED ALL THE ANIMALS

Genesis 1:25

Word Challenge

Starting with animals, how many words can you make out of
I can do everything through him who gives me strength?

mouse	toad	horse
_____	_____	_____
_____	_____	_____
_____	_____	_____
_____	_____	_____
_____	_____	_____
_____	_____	_____
_____	_____	_____
_____	_____	_____

I can do everything through him who gives me strength.
Philippians 4:13

KINDNESS

But the fruit of the Spirit is love, joy, peace, patience, kindness, goodness, faithfulness, gentleness and self-control... Galatians 5:22

Old Testament Books of the Bible Crossword

Down

1. Starts with D, ends with Y
2. Used in math
3. The letters mixed up: SOMA
4. Follows Hosea

Across

1. Ends with L
2. Sixth book of the Bible
3. Mixed up: HHEEMIAN
4. Was inside a whale
5. Follows Jeremiah
6. _____, Daniel, Hosea, Joel

PRAISE

Enter his gates with thanksgiving
and his courts with praise.
Psalm 100:4

Scripture Scramble

___ ___ ___ ___
l   n a c   o d   e v g n i g e r y t h

___ ___ ___ ___
h h r o g u t   h m i   o h w   i g e v s

___ ___
e m   t t h e n g r s   **Philippians 4:13**

Names of God Crossword

Down
1. Spoke the world into being
2. Old Testament name
3. Ends with D
4. Starts with J
5. Three in one
6. The letters mixed up: SSHMIAE
7. Means Lord, Master in Hebrew, and starts with A

Across
1. Starts with H, ends with T
2. Old Testament name, means more than enough
3. Not mother
4. Not daughter
5. Everlasting God in Hebrew. The letters mixed up: LLEOMA

IN THE BEGINNING GOD CREATED

In the beginning God created the heavens and the earth...
And God said, "Let the water teem with living creatures,..."
Genesis 1:1,20

Scripture Scramble

___ ____, ____ _____ __ ____
yM   osn   ypa   tttnnoiea   ot   tawh

_ ____; _____ _____ __ __ _____.
I   ysa   tenlis   llyscoe   ot   ym   wdrso

__ ___ ___ ____ ___ __ ____
oD   tno   tle   htme   tuo   fo   ryuo

_____, ____ ___ ____ ____
isthg   eepk   mhte   nihtiw   ouyr

_____; ___ ____ ___ ___ __
hraet   rof   htye   rae   flei   ot

_____ ___ ___ ____ ___ _____
tesoh   ohw   ndfi   meth   dna   hhltae

__ a ____'s _____ _____. Proverbs 4:20-22
ot   nma   olehw   dbyo

56

PRAY

Do not be anxious about anything, but in everything, by prayer
and petition, with thanksgiving, present your requests to God.
Philippians 4:6

Jesus Heals Word Search

```
H E A L E D Q R Z P D P J B C R K R R J R
G I O T G P F T A D L D D P T T L T A P A
R S P O P S O O J S G S R E P A J O L S I
T U D J D U S F P F P F T U A J R J E U S
G O P P S S H E S D S M O S S F S P N S E
C T F D F T F V U K U I J T F D U D F T D
A S D S D S D E E H S R P S E T K S D W D
G L K U K L K R A T V A D L K F T U K I E
E J S D S J S S B C S C S J S R S L S T A
L R T T D T T L J L L U R T E L T T H D
S L C S C E C C E V J E S D C E J C C E T
T A J S J L J S R B R S T B D S R S J R C
C M V L V I V L D R D R C T L L D B V E S
S E L J B V B J O D B D S R V J B J U D L
L P L E P E R V T C T L L P E V T V R H L
J O D B N R D B L V R S I C K B R N O A V
V R C R C E C R P X P X V N C R P R C N T
R L i O T D R D O Z O Z T N D Y K K N D D
```

How God anointed Jesus of Nazareth the Holy Spirit and power, and how he went about doing good and healing all who were under the power of the devil, because God was with him. Acts 10:38

HEALED	MIRACLES
RAISED DEAD	FEVER
DELIVERED	SICK
BLIND	LEPER
DEAF	SET FREE
LAME	WITHERED HAND

58

TAKE DELIGHT
IN THE LORD
and he will give you
the desires of your heart.

Psalm 37:4

Word Challenge

How many words can you make out of

we live by faith, not by sight?

fast		
boar		

We live by faith, not by sight. 2 Corinthians 5:7

Old Testament Books of the Bible Crossword

Down
1. The 26th book in the Bible
2. The book before Numbers
3. It follows Genesis
4. Ends with s & has much wisdom
5. The 28th book of the Bible

Across
1. ARZE backwards
2. A Queen
3. In the beginning
4. These letters mixed up: SSMALP
5. _____, Psalms, Proverbs, Ecclesiastes
6. Daniel, Hosea, _____ .

62

...BE GENEROUS AND WILLING TO SHARE.

1 Timothy 6:18

63

Scripture Challenge

Can you list the fruit of the Spirit
located in Galatians 5:22-23 before looking?

1. _____
2. _____
3. _____
4. _____
5. _____
6. _____
7. _____
8. _____
9. _____

"Love your neighbor as yourself." Love does no harm to a neighbor.
Therefore love is the fulfillment of the law.
Romans 13:9-10

Scripture Scramble

..._____ _____ _____ . 1 John 4:8
    dGo   si   vleo

_____ _____ _____ _____ _____
eGvi   anksth   ot   het   droL

_____ ____ ____ _____ ; _____ _____
orf   eh   si   gdoo   shi   elvo

_____ _____ . Psalm 118:1
neesrud   ofeevrr

66

COMPASSION AND KINDNESS

Therefore, as God's chosen people, holy and dearly loved, clothe yourselves
with compassion, kindness, humility, gentleness, and patience.
Colossians 3:12

Word Challenge

How many words can you make out of

worship the Lord your God?

dog		
ship		

Worship the Lord your God, and serve him only. Matthew 4:10

But thanks be to God!
He gives us the victory through our Lord Jesus Christ.
1 Corinthians 15:57

Scripture Scramble

_____ _____ _____ _____ "_____ _____

eH   dias   ot   hemt   oG   toin

_____ _____ _____ _____ _____ _____

lal   het   dlrow   adn   heacrp   eht

_____ _____ _____ _____ _____. _____

dogo   wesn   ot   lal   noitaerc.   reveohW

_____ _____ _____ _____ _____

seeevilb   dna   si   pabzidet   lwil

_____ _____...."   Mark 16:15-16

eb   vaesd

70

Word Challenge

How many words can you make out of
love is patient, love is kind...love never fails?

__kindness__   _____   _____

_____   _____   _____

_____   _____   _____

_____   _____   _____

_____   _____   _____

_____   _____   _____

_____   _____   _____

_____   _____   _____

_____   _____   _____

Love is patient, love is kind. It does not envy, it does not boast, it is not proud. It is not rude, it is not self-seeking, it is not easily angered, it keeps no record of wrongs. Love does not delight in evil but rejoices with the truth. It always trusts, always hopes, always perseveres. Love never fails. 1 Corinthians 13:4-8

GOD CREATED

the great creatures of the sea
and every living thing
with which the water teems
and that moves about in it...
Genesis 1:21

Scripture Scramble

"Have faith in God," Jesus answered. "I tell you the truth, if anyone says to this mountain, 'Go throw yourself into the sea,' and does not doubt in his heart but believes that what he says will happen, it will be done for him.

_____ | ____ ____
eeerrfTho   l   ellt   uoy

_____ ____ ___ ___ __
aevewhtr   uoy   ska   rof   ni

_____ _____ ____ ___ ____
reyarp   ebleevi   ttah   ouy   eavh

_____ __ ___ __ ____
deeevcri   ti   dna   ti   llwi

___ _____.   Mark 11:22-24
eb   sruoy

"...WITH GOD ALL THINGS ARE POSSIBLE."

Matthew 19:26

Word Challenge

How many words can you make out of

Love the Lord your God with all your heart?

heat

great

_____   _____   _____

**Love the LORD your God with all your heart and with all your soul
and with all your strength. Deuteronomy 6:5**

God is love

1 John 4:16

PRAY

If you remain in me and my words remain in you,
ask whatever you wish, and it will be done for you.
John 15:7

PRAY AND GIVE THANKS

Do not be anxious about anything, but in every situation, by prayer and petition, with thanksgiving, present your requests to God. And the peace of God, which transcends all understanding, will guard your hearts and your minds in Christ Jesus.
Philippians 4:6-7

PRAY AND BELIEVE

Therefore I tell you, whatever you ask for in prayer,
believe that you have received it, and it will be yours.
Mark 11:24

ANSWERS

ANSWERS

Animals in the Bible Crossword

Across
1. Swallowed Jonah
2. Peter denied Jesus then...
3. Rise Peter kill and eat (God made clean)
4. Bird
5. The wise men rode on a _____

Down
1. Baby sheep
2. Jesus rode on a _____
3. Needs a shepherd.
4. Prepares for winter, called wise in Proverbs 6:6.
5. Daniel killed one.
6. Likes climbing mountains.
7. Type of black bird
8. Returned to Noah with an olive branch.
9. _____ of Judah.

```
                                         5
                                        [B]
                          4             [E]
                 2       [A]            [A]
                [D]      [N]            [N]
          2 [R][O][O][S][T][E][R]                        8
                [N]   3  [H]                             [D]
          1     [K]      [E]              7              [O]
    1    [L]    [E]      [E]             [R]             [V]  9
   [W][H][A][L][E]       [E]   6    5 [C][A][M][E][L]   [L]
         [M]    [Y]    3 [P][I][G]     [A]              [I]
         [B]            [O]            [V]              [O]
                     4 [E][A][G][L][E] [E]              [N]
                        [T]            [N]
```

83

Answers to page 2

Love is ...
Word Search

```
H J U R G J Q R Z P D P J B C R K R R J N
G I O T G P F T A D A D D P T T L T A P H
R S P O P S O O J S G S R P P A J O L S A
T U D J D U S J P F T A D J R J E U K
G O P P S S H P S D R D O T S P S K I N D
C T F D F T F D U K O K J I F D U D F T S
A S D S D S R S E H T S P E D S K S P S H
G L K U K L E U A T E T D N N U T U D L I
E J S D S J J S C C C S T E S S L P J E
L R T T T R O T L T T J U R V T N T E R P
S D C S C D I F E V S V S D E C O C R D S
L N J S J B C A R B R B T B R S T S S B T
C O V L V T E I D R D R C T F L P B E T C
S T V J B R S T O D B D S R A J R J V R S
L R R E R P R H T C T C L P I V O V E F L
J U D B N O D B L H O P E O L B U N R O L
V D C R C B C R P X P X V R S R D R E R V
R E O S T E R D O Z O Z T N O Y K K S O D
```

Love is patient, love is kind...Love never fails. 1 Corinthians 13:4-8

LOVE
FAITH
HOPE
PATIENT
KIND
NOT RUDE

REJOICES
PROTECTS
TRUSTS
PERSEVERES
NOT PROUD
NEVER FAILS

Answers to page 4

Scripture Scramble

How great is the love the Father has lavished on us, that we should be called children of God! And that is what we are! 1 John 3:1

How	great	is	the	love	the
o H w	t g e a r	s i	e h t	v e l o	e h t

Father	has	lavished	on	us
F r e a t h	a s h	d e h s i v a l	n o	s u

that	we	should	be	called
t t a h	e w	d l u o h s	e b	l l a e d c

children	of	God	!	And	that
n e r d l i h c	f o	o d G		n d A	h a t t

is	what	we	are	!	1 John 3:1
s i	t a h w	e w	r e a		

85

Answers to page 6

Word Challenge

How many words can you make out of

trust in the Lord?

hen	dirt	hot
tent	end	let
rust	lend	line
tin	tend	tint
stilt	dine	dent
lend	lit	rent
then	hide	sin
thin	dot	ride
thrust	net	rode
dust	lot	tot

Trust in the LORD with all your heart and lean not on your own
understanding; in all your ways acknowledge him,
and he will make your paths straight. Proverbs 3:5-6

Answers to page 8

Books of the Bible Crossword

Across
1. The letters mixed up: hiiiPPPlans
2. The 17th book of the New Testament
3. The book before Revelations
4. Between Ephesians and Timothy
5. The letters mixed up: aaasnitlg

Down
1. Starts with P, ends with n
2. Follows Ezekiel
3. Two books before Colossians
4. Follows Philemon

Answers to page 10

Compassion Word Search

```
H K U R G J Q R L O V P J B C R K R R J N
G I O T L P F T A D T D D P T G R A C E H
R K P I O S I O J S G S R S P A J O L S A
T I D J V U S J P F P F T U D J B J E U K
G N P M S S H P S D S D O S S P S L N S E
C D F D E T F D U F L L J T F D U D E T S
A N D S D R D S E O S S O S D S K S D S H
G E K U K L C U A R V T D V K U T U K L S
E S S C J S Y B G S C S J E S S L S J E
L S T O T R T T L I L J U R T T L T T R P
S D C M C D C C E V J V S D C C J G C D S
T B J P J B J S R E B T B D S R E J B T
C T V A V T V L D N D R C T L L D N V T C
S R L S E R V E O E B D S R V J B E U R S
L P R S R P R V T S T C L P E V T R R F L
J O D I N O D B L S R V J O D B R O O L
V R C O C B C R P X P X V R C R P U C R V
R L O N T E R D O Z O Z T N O Y K S N O D
```

GRACE
MERCY
COMPASSION
FORGIVENESS
LOVE
GENEROUS
BLESS
SERVE
KINDNESS

The Lord is full of compassion and mercy. James 5:11

88   Answers to page 12

Scripture Scramble

But the fruit of the Spirit is love, joy, peace, patience, kindness, goodness, faithfulness, gentleness and self-control. Galatians 5:22-23

But	the	fruit	of	the	Spirit	is
t B u	h e t	t i u r f	f o	e t h	t i i r p S	s i

love , joy , peace , patience ,
v e l o   o y j   a p e e c   e c n e t a p i

kindness , goodness , faithfulness ,
n e s s d n k i   n o o s s e g d   s s f f e u a n l t h i

gentleness and self - control .
e e e s s n n l t g   n a d   l e s f   o o n r t l c

Galatians 5:22-23

Answers to page 14

Word Challenge

How many words can you make out of

we are God's workmanship?

man	ape	pig
sweep	him	weak
ship	make	grip
dog	rake	more
worm	rear	grow
swim	ear	row
good	whip	win
work	when	rip
hip	where	dip
wig	week	dig

For we are God's workmanship, created in Christ Jesus to do good works, which God prepared in advance for us to do. Ephesians 2:10

Answers to page 16

Noah's Ark Crossword

Across
1. Pets
2. Who built the ark?
3. Another word for promise.
4. What book of the Bible says God created the animals?
5. Hebrews 11:7 By _____ Noah...

Down
1. Came with a promise
2. Huge animal
3. Boat
4. Like a big cat

1. r
   a n i m a l s
   i
2. N o a h
   b
3. c o v e n a n t
   w l r
     e k
     p
5. f a i t h
     a
4. G e n e s i s
     t

(down 2) l e p h a n t
(down 4) l i o n

Answers to page 18

Think on These Things
Word Search

```
H J U R G J Q R Z P D P J B C R K R R J N
G I O T G P F T A D E N D P T T L T A P H
R S P I P S I O R S G S O S P A J O L S A
T U D J D U S J P U P F T B D J R J E U K
G O P P S S H P S D E D O S L P U R E S P
C T T D F T F D U K X K J T F E U D F T R
A S H S D S D S E H C S P S D A K S D S A
G L I U K L K U A T E T D L K C T U K L I
E J N D S J S S B C L C S J S E S L S J S
L R K T T A T T L J L J U R T O L T T R E
S D C S C D C C E V E V S D C F J C C D W
T B J S J M J S R B N B T B D G R S J B O
C T V L V I V R D R T R C L L O D B V T R
S R L J B R B J I D D D S O V D B J U R T
L P R A R A R V T G B C L V E V T V R F H
J O D B N B D B L V H V J E D B R N O O Y
V R C R C L C R P X R T V L C R P R C R C
R L O I T E R D O Z P Z T Y O Y K K N O O
```

Finally, brothers, whatever is true, whatever is noble, whatever is right, whatever is pure, whatever is lovely, whatever is admirable – if anything Is excellent or praiseworthy – think about such things. Philippians 4:8

TRUE   ADMIRABLE
NOBLE   EXCELLENT
RIGHT   PRAISEWORTHY
PURE   PEACE OF GOD
LOVELY   THINK

Answers to page 20

Scripture Scramble

Do not let this Book of the Law depart from your mouth; meditate on it day and night, so that you may be careful to do everything written in it. Then you will be prosperous and successful. Joshua 1:8

Do   **not**   **let**   **this**   **Book**   **of**   **the**
o D   o t n   t e l   t h s i   k B o o   f o   e t h

Law   **depart**   **from**   **your**   **mouth** ;
L w a   t r a p e d   r m o f   r y u o   t h m o u

meditate   **on**   **it**   **day**   **and**   **night** ,
e t t i d e m a   n o   t i   y a d   n a d   g h t n i

so   **that**   **you**   **may**   **be**   **careful**
o s   t t a h   u o y   y m a   e b   e c a r l u f

to   **do**   **everything**   **written**   **in**
o t   o d   g n h t y r v i e e   r w e n t t i   n i

it .   **Then**   **you**   **will**   **be**
t i   n e T h   o u y   l i w l   e b

prosperous   **and**   **successful** .   Joshua 1:8
s s u o o r r e p p   d n a   f u l s s s c c e u

Answers to page 22

Word Challenge

How many words can you make out of

forgive others?

frog	hot	fight
for	rig	goof
forge	fig	gift
got	fit	sift
forth	fort	soft
five	give	rot
get	those	hog
their	ever	fog
there	grieve	river
here	right	toe

For if you forgive men when they sin against you, your heavenly Father will also forgive you. But if you do not forgive men their sins, your Father will not forgive your sins. Matthew 6:14-15

94

Answers to page 24

Books of the Bible Crossword

Down
1. Mixed up: SNAMOR
2. Ends with S
3. Mixed up: SSSAANNIOLHTE
4. Follows Romans

Across
1. Last book of the Bible
2. Starts with T
3. Starts with J
4. Disciple walked on water
5. Matthew, Mark, Luke, ___

Answers to page 26

Joshua 1:8 Word Search

```
B J U R G J Q R Z P D P J O C R K R R J T
I I O T G P F T A D E D D B T T L T A P W
B S P I P S I O J S G S R E P A J O L S R
L U D J D N S J P E V E R Y T J R J E U I
G O P P S S I P S D S D O S H P S P N S T
C T F D F T F G U K U K J T I D U D F T T
A S D S D S D S H H S S P S N S K S D S E
G L K U K B K U A T V T D L G U T U P L N
E J S D S I S S B C S C S J T S S L R J I
L R T T T B T T L J L J U R C T U T O R M
S D C S C L C C H V J V S D D C C S D E
T B J S J E J J R E R B T B L S C S P B D
C T V L V T V O D R N R C T V L E B E T I
S R L J B R B S O D B D S R E J S J R R T
L P R A R P R H T C T C L P D V S V O F A
D O D B N O D U L V R V J O C B F N U O T
V A C R C B C A P X P X V R O R U R S R E
R L Y I T E R D O Z O Z T N T Y L K T O L
```

Do not let this Book of the Law depart from your mouth; meditate on it day and night, so that you may be careful to do everything written in it. Then you will be prosperous and successful. Joshua 1:8

BIBLE
MEDITATE
DAY
NIGHT
OBEY
EVERYTHING

WRITTEN
THEN
PROSPEROUS
SUCCESSFUL
JOSHUA

Answers to page 28

Scripture Scramble

That if you confess with your mouth, "Jesus is Lord," and believe in your heart that God raised him from the dead, you will be saved. Romans 10:9

<u>That</u>	<u>if</u>	<u>you</u>	<u>confess</u>	<u>with</u>
T t a h	f i	o u y	f e s s c o n	i t h w

<u>your</u>	<u>mouth</u> ,	<u>"Jesus</u>	<u>is</u>	<u>Lord,"</u>
r u o y	t h o u m	s s J u e	s i	d r o L

<u>and</u>	<u>believe</u>	<u>in</u>	<u>your</u>	<u>heart</u>
d n a	e e e l b i v	n i	u o r y	a r t h e

<u>that</u>	<u>God</u>	<u>raised</u>	<u>him</u>	<u>from</u>
h a t t	d o G	a s i e d r	m i h	o m f r

<u>the</u>	<u>dead</u>	<u>you</u>	<u>will</u>	<u>be</u>
h t e	a e d d	u o y	l l w i	e b

<u>saved.</u>	Romans 10:9
d a v e s	

97

Answers to page 30

Word Challenge

How many words can you make out of
therefore love is the fulfillment of the law?

lion	feet	swift
here	train	fall
fill	tame	tall
leaf	lame	small
lease	lost	hall
fast	host	mall
last	most	malt
least	toast	shall
firm	roast	shout
fame	those	frame

"Love your neighbor as yourself." Love does no harm to its neighbor.
Therefore love is the fulfillment of the law. Romans 13:9-10

98

Answers to page 32

Apostles Crossword

Down
1. Doubting _____
2. Starts with B
3. Gave Jesus a kiss

Across
1. He wrote "the disciple Jesus loved"
2. Starts with A, ends ends with W
3. The letters mixed up: DDAAEUSHT
4. Another name for Peter
5. In the book of _____ we're told to control our tongue.
6. The first book of the New Testament.

1 Down: T o m a s (across: J o h n)
2 Down: B r h h (across: A n d r e w)
3 Across: T h a d d a e u s
3 Down: J u d a s
4 Across: S I m o N
5 Across: J a m e S
6 Across: M a t t h e w

Answers to page 34

Genesis Chapter 1
Word Search

```
H J U R G J Q R Z P D P J B C R K A R J N
G O D T G P F T A E V E D P T G L T D P H
R S P O P S O O J S G S R L P A J O L A A
T U D J D U S J P F P F N A D R R J E C M
G O P P S S H P S D S D I N S D S P N R E
C T F D F T F D U K G K G T F E U D F E S
A S D S D S D S G H E S H S D N K S D A H
G L K U D L K U O T N T J G U T U K T I
E J S D S A S S O C E S R O S S L S E E
L R T T T R Y T D J S J U D D T L C T D P
R D C S C L C C D V I V S B S C J R C D S
U B J S J I J S O B S B T T A S R E J G T
L T V L V K V L T R D R C R I L D A V E C
E R L J B E B I L D B D S I D J B T U N S
O P R A R N R G L C T I L P D V T U R E L
V O D B N E D H L V R V R O C B R R O S L
E R C R C S C T P X P X V D O R P E C I V
R F I S H S R D I M A G E N S Y K S N S D
```

GOD

RULE OVER

CREATED

FISH

ADAM

BIRDS

EVE

CREATURES

GARDEN

PLANTS

GOD SAID

DAY

LIGHT

NIGHT

IMAGE

GOOD

LIKENESS

GENESIS

Answers to page 36

Scripture Scramble

Finally, brothers, whatever is true, whatever is noble, whatever is right, whatever is pure, whatever is lovely, whatever is admirable—if anything is excellent or praiseworthy– think about such things. Philippians 4:8

Finally, **brothers** **whatever** **is**
F l l y a i n   s r e t h r o b   e e a r v t h w   s i

true, **whatever** **is** **noble**,
e r u t   r e v e t a h w   s i   o e n b l

whatever **is** **right**, **whatever**
t w h r v e e a   s i   g t h r i   r a e e v w h t

is **pure**, **whatever** **is** **lovely**
s i   u e r p   e e a r v t h w   s i   e y l v l o

whatever **is** **admirable** - **if**
r e v e w h t a   s i   e l b a r i m a d   f i

anything **is** **excellent** **or**
y g n n t h a i   s i   e e e l l x c t n   r o

praiseworthy - **think** **about** **such** **things**
y t h r o w p e i s a r   t k i n h   a t b u o   h c u s   g s n h t i

Philippians 4:8

Answers to page 38

Word Challenge

How many words can you make out of

with God all things are possible?

dog	bone	star
swing	twins	ball
tree	bear	sweet
rings	bare	open
nest	sing	going
hen	whine	ten
swollen	win	pin
greet	gossip	swine
great	sew	pig
hospitable	thin	soap

Jesus looked at them and said, "With man this is impossible, but with God all things are possible." Matthew 19:26

Answers to page 40

New Testament Books of the Bible Crossword

Down
1. Starts with M
2. Ends with S
3. _____, Philemon, Hebrews, James
4. The 65th book of the Bible

Across
1. Ends with K
2. Follows the book of John
3. Before the book of Acts
4. A language plus S
5. Gospels, Acts, _____
6. Starts with G

```
                                                              3 [T]
      1                                        2            
      [M][A][R][K]                             [E]            [I]
         [A]                                   [P]            [T]
    2 [A][C][T]_[S]              3             [H]   ■       [U]
         [T] ■  ■ [H][E][B][R][E][W][S]
    4 [J][O][H][N]                             [S]
      [U]    [E]                               [I]
      [D]    [W]                  5 [R][O][M][A][N][S]
      [E]                                ■   [N]
    6 [G][A][L][A][T][I][A][N][S]
```

103

Answers to page 42

Faith Word Search

```
H J U H G J Q R Z W A L K B Y F A I T H N
E H O E G P F T A D A D D P T T L T A P O
B S P O P S O O J S G S R S P A J O L S T
R U D J D U S J P F P F H U D J R J E U B
G H P P S S H P S D S T P S J P S P N S Y
C E F D F T F D U K I K L T F E U D F T S
A B D S D S E S E A S S E W D S S D S I
G R K U K L V U F T V T A O K U T U K L G
E E S D S J I S B C S A S R S S S L S J H
L W T T T R D T L J L B E D T T L T T S T
S S C S C D E C E V J R S O C C J C C U S
T B J S J B N S R B R A G F D S R E J B T
C T V L V T C L D R D H O G L L D R V S W
S R L J B R E J O D B A D O V J B T U T S
L P R A R P R V T C T M L D E V T A R A L
H O P E N O D B L V R V J O D B R I O N L
V R C R C B C R P X P X V R C R P N C C V
R L O S T E R D O Z O Z T N O Y K K N E W
```

Now faith is being sure of what we hope for and certain of what we do not see. Hebrews 11:1

FAITH   HOPE
HEBREWS   CERTAIN
WORD OF GOD   SUBSTANCE
PLEASES GOD   EVIDENCE
WALK BY FAITH JESUS
NOT BY SIGHT   ABRAHAM

104

Answers to page 44

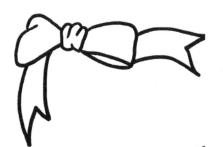

Scripture Scramble

Be kind and compassionate to one another, forgiving each other, just as in Christ God forgave you. Ephesians 4:32

Be	kind	and	compassionate
e B	d k i n	n d a	p a s s a t e i o n c o m

to	one	another	,	forgiving
o t	n o e	o t h e r a n		r o g g i i v n f

each	other	,	just	as	in
a e h c	t h o r e		t j u s	s a	n i

Christ	God	forgave	you	.
s C r h t i	o G d	e v a g r o f	o u y	

Ephesians 4:32

Answers to page 46

Word Challenge

Starting with animals, how many words can you make out of
I can do everything through him who gives me strength?

mouse	toad	horse
worm	cat	teeth
crow	dairy	strong
hog	tune	wrong
rat	mice	ring
dog	seven	stand
goat	road	hat
hen	gave	good
coot	smog	carry
tiger	mat	hair

I can do everything through him who gives me strength.
Philippians 4:13

Answers to page 48

Old Testament Books of the Bible Crossword

Down
1. Starts with D, ends with Y
2. Used in math
3. The letters mixed up: SOMA
4. Follows Hosea

Across
1. Ends with L
2. Sixth book of the Bible
3. Mixed up: HHEEMIAN
4. Was inside a whale
5. Follows Jeremiah
6. ____, Daniel, Hosea, Joel

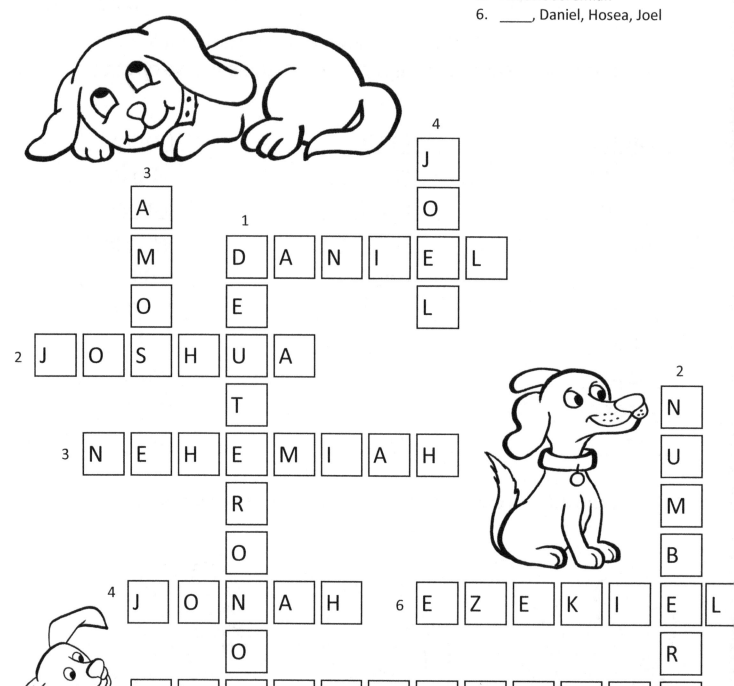

Answers to page 50

Scripture Scramble

I can do everything through him who gives me strength. Philippians 4:13

__I__	__can__	__do__	__everything__
I	n a c	o d	e v g n i g e r y t h

__through__	__him__	__who__	__gives__
h h r o g u t	h m i	o h w	i g e v s

__me__	__strength__	
e m	t t h e n g r s	**Philippians 4:13**

Answers to page 52

Names of God Crossword

Down

1. Spoke the world into being
2. Old Testament name
3. Ends with D
4. Starts with J
5. Three in one
6. The letters mixed up: SSHMIAE
7. Means Lord, Master in Hebrew, and starts with A

Across

1. Starts with H, ends with T
2. Old Testament name, means more than enough
3. Not mother
4. Not daughter
5. Everlasting God in Hebrew. The letters mixed up: LLEOMA

109

Answers to page 54

Scripture Scramble

My son, pay attention to what I say; listen closely to my words. Do not let them out of your sight, keep them within your heart; for they are life to those who find them and health to a man's whole body. Proverbs 4:20-22

My	**son** ,	**pay**	**attention**	**to**	**what**
y M	o s n	y p a	t t t n n o i e a	o t	t a w h

I	**say** ;	**listen**	**closely**	**to**	**my**	**words** .
I	y s a	t e n l i s	l l y s c o e	o t	y m	w d r s o

Do	**not**	**let**	**them**	**out**	**of**	**your**
o D	t n o	t l e	h t m e	t u o	f o	r y u o

sight ,	**keep**	**them**	**within**	**your**
i s t h g	e e p k	m h t e	n i h t i w	o u y r

heart ;	**for**	**they**	**are**	**life**	**to**
h r a e t	r o f	h t y e	r a e	f l e i	o t

those	**who**	**find**	**them**	**and**	**health**
t e s o h	o h w	n d f i	m e t h	d n a	h h l t a e

to	a	**man** 's	**whole**	**body** .	Proverbs 4:20-22
o t	n m a	o l e h w	d b y o		

Answers to page 56

Jesus Heals Word Search

```
H E A L E D Q R Z P D P J B C R K R R J R
G I O T G P F T A D L D D P T T L T A P A
R S P O P S O O J S G S R E P A J O L S I
T U D J D U S F P F P F T U A J R J E U S
G O P P S S H E S D S M O S S F S P N S E
C T F D F T F V U K U I J T F D U D F T D
A S D S D S D E E H S R P S E T K S D W D
G L K U K L R A T V A D L K F T U K I I E
E J S D S J S S B C S C J S R S L S T A D
L R T T T D T T L J L U R T E L T T H A D
S L C S C E C C E V J E S D C E J C C E T
T A J S J L J S R B R S T B D S R S J R C
C M V L V I V L D R D R C T L L D B V E S
S E L J B V B J O D B D S R V J B J U D L
L P L E P E R V T C T L L P E V T V R H L
J O D B N R D B L V R S I C K B R N O A V
V R C R C E C R P X P X V N C R P R C N T
R L O O T D R D O Z O Z T N D Y K K N D D
```

How God anointed Jesus of Nazareth with the Holy Spirit and power, and how he went about doing good and healing all who were under the power of the devil, because God was with him. Acts 10:38

HEALED	MIRACLES
RAISED DEAD	FEVER
DELIVERED	SICK
BLIND	LEPER
DEAF	SET FREE
LAME	WITHERED HAND

111

Answers to page 58

Word Challenge

How many words can you make out of

we live by faith, not by sight?

fast	bat	height
bait	hen	hat
life	tent	get
bite	light	lived
bath	tight	base
hive	tenth	waste
when	west	vase
fight	wing	eight
night	last	ate
life	low	test

We live by faith, not by sight. 2 Corinthians 5:7

112   Answers to page 60

Old Testament Books of the Bible Crossword

Down
1. The 26th book in the Bible
2. The book before Numbers
3. It follows Genesis
4. Ends with s & has much wisdom
5. The 28th book of the Bible

Across
1. ARZE backwards
2. A Queen
3. In the beginning
4. These letters mixed up: SSMALP
5. _____, Psalms, Proverbs, Ecclesiastes
6. Daniel, Hosea, _____ .

Answers to page 62

Scripture Challenge

Can you list the fruit of the Spirit
located in Galatians 5:22-23 before looking?

1. __love__
2. __joy__
3. __peace__
4. __patience__
5. __kindness__
6. __goodness__
7. __faithfulness__
8. __gentleness__
9. __self-control__

But the fruit of the Spirit is love, joy, peace, patience, kindness, goodness, faithfulness, gentleness and self-control. Galatians 5:22-23

Answers to page 64

Scripture Scramble

...God is love. 1John 4:8.
Give thanks to the Lord for he is good;
his love endures forever. Psalm 118:1

... __God__ __is__ __love__ . 1 John 4:8
    d G o   s i   v l e o

__Give__ __thanks__ __to__ __the__ __Lord__
e G v i   a n k s t h   o t   h e t   d r o L

__for__ __he__ __is__ __good__ ; __his__ __love__
o r f   e h   s i   g d o o   s h i   e l v o

__endures__ __forever__ . Psalm 118:1
n e e s r u d   o f e e v r r

Answers to page 66

Word Challenge

How many words can you make out of

worship the Lord your God?

dog	rip	hope
ship	grip	lip
sip	pole	soul
good	hole	their
door	hide	wig
hoop	ride	pig
loop	slide	rig
poor	glide	tip
swipe	this	our
wipe	rode	out

Worship the Lord your God, and serve him only. Matthew 4:10

Answers to page 68

Scripture Scramble

He said to them, "Go into all the world and preach the good news to all creation. Whoever believes and is baptized will be saved..."
Mark 16:15-16

__He__	__said__	__to__	__them,__	__"Go__	__into__
e H	d i a s	o t	h e m t	o G	t o i n

__all__	__the__	__world__	__and__	__preach__	__the__
l a l	h e t	d l r o w	a d n	h r e a c p	e h t

__good__	__news__	__to__	__all__	__creation.__	__Whoever__
d o g o	w e s n	o t	l a l	n o i t a e r c .	r e v e o h W

__believes__	__and__	__is__	__baptized__	__will__
s e e e v i l b	d n a	s i	p a b z i d e t	l w i l

__be__	__saved__ ..."	**Mark 16:15-16**
e b	v a e s d	

117   Answers to page 70

Word Challenge

How many words can you make out of

love is patient, love is kind...love never fails?

kindness	paint	pet
lion	petal	let
tent	nap	ton
lend	leper	ten
find	letter	pole
kettle	event	send
settle	viper	faint
net	tap	save
dollar	toast	tend
dolls	dove	fever

Love is patient, love is kind. It does not envy, it does not boast, it is not proud. It is not rude, it is not self-seeking, it is not easily angered, it keeps no record of wrongs. Love does not delight in evil but rejoices with the truth. It always trusts, always hopes, always perseveres. Love never fails. 1 Corinthians 13:4-8

Answers to page 72

Scripture Scramble

"Have faith in God," Jesus answered. "I tell you the truth, if anyone says to this mountain, 'Go throw yourself into the sea,' and does not doubt in his heart but believes that what he says will happen, it will be done for him.

Therefore	I	tell	you
e e e r r f T h o	I	e l l t	u o y

whatever	you	ask	for	in
a e v e w h t r	u o y	s k a	r o f	n i

prayer	believe	that	you	have
r e y a r p	e b l e e v i	t t a h	o u y	e a v h

recieved	it	and	it	will
d e e e v c r i	t i	d n a	t i	l l w i

be	yours	.	Mark 11:22-24
e b	s r u o y		

Therefore I tell you, whatever you ask for in prayer, believe that you have received it, and it will be yours. Mark 11: 22-24

119

Answers to page 74

Word Challenge

How many words can you make out of

Love the Lord your God with all your heart?

heat	dove	tag
great	late	rag
true	tea	tart
good	will	drag
hood	hall	youth
tall	log	twig
wall	dog	wig
doll	wag	loot
rat	hey	lot
that	goal	roll

Love the LORD your God with all your heart and with all your soul and with all your strength. Deuteronomy 6:5

Answers to page 76

Books by GiGi Allen

(Available on Amazon.com)

The Creative Power of Your Words
Bible Highlights
Walking with God (a study guide)
How to Get to Heaven

Books for Children:
Scriptures To Color Volumes 1-8, with reproducible pages
Scriptures To Color Volumes 2-5 in Spanish with reproducible pages
Ucan the Toucan (a story book to color)
How To Draw (Cartoons for Beginners)
My First Animal Coloring Book
My Alphabet Coloring Book
The Best Bible Activity Book (with fun-filled reproducible pages)
The Best Bible Coloring & Activity Book (fun-filled reproducible pages)

About the Author/Illustrator

GiGi Allen is a pastor, author and illustrator. An ordained minister and a graduate of Rhema Bible College, she holds a B.A. degree in advertising with a minor in business. She served as a children's minister for many years, and has pastored, along with her husband for the past 18 years at Victory International Church in San Mateo, CA. (www.victoryic.org). She has also served as dean and as an instructor of Victory Bible School. Pastor GiGi continues to minister overseas, taking the gospel to the nations. Her passion is to equip the saints for the work of service, through teaching and impartation.

Made in the USA
Monee, IL
17 February 2020